How to Start a Photography Business

A Beginner's Guide to A Successful Career as A Photographer

Maxwell Rotheray

Table of Contents

CHAPTER ONE:

Introduction

Photography business looks easy, and of course, it is easy. If you have a smartphone and use it to capture images of yourself or something else, you are already a photographer. I am a photographer; you are, most of us are. However, being a photographer in business is completely a different ball game since you are there to make a profit. It requires a huge investment in training, equipment purchases and a long period of exposure in the art of photography for anyone to succeed in the business.

Let me introduce you in this book different areas of the photography business, and you can select the one that suits your purpose.

On the face of it, it may look easy to make a career in photography, simply because anybody can be a photographer. But it is not as easy as it looks since it is not just to set up as a photographer, you have to grow and sustain your business in the foreseeable future

It may sound untrue, but an estimated 60% of those who went into photography business lasted for less than one year before folding up, and still another 25% did not hit the two-year mark before they closed down.

So, if you want to succeed in this noble profession, you must work hard and sustain your hard work for a long time.

CHAPTER TWO

Different Types of Photography

1. Landscape photography

Like nature and want to capture beautiful scenery out there, whether, at the seaside or mountain top, you are into landscape photography.

2. Wildlife photography

Mostly at a professional level or on assignment, the photographer captures animals, there interaction with each other, and how they adapt to new environment. It also captures their behaviors in natural habitats in comparison to strength and structural advantages. Exhibitions, journals and magazines are the perfect homes for nature or wildlife pictures.

3. Aerial photography

Certain places cannot be easily captured such as dangerous rivers or lakes that stretch a long distance; such places can only be captured from a higher altitude such as airplanes, air balloons, parachutes, and skyscrapers. The larger view of the subject and its background is better provided.

4. Sports photography

This genre of photography captures action movement in sports events, such as horse racing or motor racing. It is among the high paying and adventurous types of photography. You will enjoy this type of photography if you focus on sports of interest and follow trends.

5. Portrait photography

This is the oldest type of photography which can include capturing members of your immediate family or friends and posting it on social media.

6. Architectural photography

Focused on buildings, houses, and structures, angling is essential in partaking on architectural photography. The essence is to create a positive impact on potential purchasers of property.

7. Event photography

This type captures events such as weddings, anniversary or company annual general meeting.

8. Fashion photography

Fashion magazines and advertising practitioners engage photographers to capture models in glamorous light display and fashion items such as clothes, hats, watches, shoes and other attractive clothing accessories.

9. Beauty photography

This type of photography is mainly to bring out the real beauty in the subjects, and it requires great skill from the photographer.

10. Bird photography

For lovers of nature, love photography can also be adventurous. It gives you the chance to travel, and you will have the opportunity to obtain rare angles. The demand for bird photographers is more than people often imagine. It is part of nature photography that captures the mood and great sceneries.

11. Black and white photography

This is still trending despite being overtaken by color pictures since it helps to bring out the natural beauty of the subject matter.

12. Candid photography

Candid photography comprises capturing pictures taken in completely natural states of the subject without any previous preparedness.

13. Firework photography

This type of photography does not require highly skilled to use the camera since the normal camera can be used in operation.

14. Food photography

If you love cooking, this type of photography will be a great choice. Even if you don't know how to cook, having an interest in different kinds of dishes is enough reason to step foot into food photography. Supermarkets and grocery stores make extensive use of this type of photography in promoting their trade.

15. Mobile photography

This type of photography was developed when cameras were first integrated into mobile phones, and today it appears to be the most popular types of photography since most people use smartphones.

16. Modeling photography

Today models are very important for existing product display and even for the launching of new product in the market. Being a modeling photographer means you have o work with models in showcasing the beauty and bringing out the best in the product, that will aid in sales and marketing.

17. Pet photography

If you like pets such as cats, dogs or birds, you can keep on capturing them.

As you can see, you can make up your mind on the aspect of photography that meets your requirements. Any aspect of photography business you choose, it requires a lot of efforts, with the right equipment and the passion for succeeding, the sky is surely your limit.

At this stage, let me introduce you to the types of equipment you need to start your photography business with. They are many, but you need not to purchase all at the same time.

CHAPTER THREE

Equipment to Start A Photographic Business

1. Camera

Obviously, the most important equipment to a photographer, professional or not, is a camera. Some work better than others in certain situations than others; you must find out which one is best suited for your purpose and your niche.

2. Tripod

This is a piece of important equipment since it makes it possible for you to take photographs of the subject without moving the camera around.

3. Camera bag

You need to protect your camera particularly when you are moving it from one place to another; you need a camera bag.

4. Lighting

Studio lighting is essential when you don't have sufficient of the natural sunlight.

5. Lenses

To get different types of images, you need different types of lenses so that you can improve the quality of your pictures.

6. Backdrops

The background where the photograph is taken determines the quality of the pictures so you have to buy or create some backdrops that you can use for studio or portrait photographs

7. Props

To display your photographs well to catch the eyes of your prospects, you need varieties of Props. So, you may have to invest in them.

8. Studio Space

Depending on your size, you need to lease or buy a studio space for your photography business.

9. Transportation

If you need to visit your clients to take photographs, you need to have a reliable means of transportation so that you don't miss deadlines.

10. An upgraded smartphone with a great camera.

In the alternative, you can have a smartphone handy which you can occasionally use to take photographs you can share on the social media.

11. Editing software

The editing software enables you to fine-tune your images. Programs like photoshop is a good investment for photographers

12. Computer systems

You get yourself a desktop or Laptop which you use for editing and the storage of your digital photos.

13. Mobile Photography Apps

These applications help you fine-tune and improve your mobile photos.

14. Social media channels

To share your photos on social media channels such as Instagram or Facebook, you need to sign up for the accounts.

15. Domain Name

A professional website or blog can be a helpful tool for a photography business, to create the one that suits your brand or business.

16. Online/Web Authority

It can benefit you to showcase your photography business on your website or blog or other locations online.

17. Call cards

This is an easy way to get in touch when you go to jobs or interact with clients.

18. Accounting programs

You need to keep a track record of your finances, invest in accounting program or professional accountant.

19. Payment Platform

You need to design how to collect your payment online, so you set up a payment system online or have a mobile payment platform to offer clients.

20. External Hard Drive

Digital photos can take a lot of space on your hard drive; you should invest in an external flash drive.

21. Business license

it isn't a bad idea to formalize your business by registering it with the local or state government. Find out the licenses that are necessary for the photography business.

22. Insurance

Moreover, you must have an insurance policy that covers your photographic equipment in case they get damaged or stolen.

23. PPA Membership

The professional photographers of America is an association of professional photographers that provides resources to its members such as industry data and contract samples.

Before introducing you into the art of photography proper, let up sum up the likely amount of money it will cost you to start a photography business.

CHAPTER FOUR

The Cost of Starting A Photography Business

In determining costs, it is advisable to write down your goals first. Determine whether you want to start at home, open a commercial photography studio, or travel. This will bring the cost of an apartment, needed equipment, and whether you have to employ someone or not. The amount of money required for starting the business is not fixed neither does it depend on your budget. It is advisable to start small and grow over time than to start big. The risks associated with the photography business is not minute so every effort must be made to reduce the start-up costs. The detailed cost to be incurred by anybody going into photography business in the United States are as follows:

I. Business registration:

It is absolutely necessary to formalize your photography business from the onset by registering it with the appropriate authority. In the US, every state has its own rules, so it is important to find out from the state you intend to operate from the cost of business registration or incorporation. On average, the cost of business registration should not be more than $135, but you must also take up insurance cover for your business. In the US, $550 for one calendar year is the estimated insurance price. You must endeavor to follow the due process in getting your photography business off to a good start so that you are always on the right side of the law. Total = $685

II. Cost of setting up your studio and renting your facility

An average facility for your studio should be about $1,600 per annum but can be less in some states in the United States. In addition, you will have to set up your studio, and the setup cost should not be around $550 or more. Total = $2,150

III. Cost of two standard cameras

As a photographer, one of your basic working tools is the camera, and you must try to buy a minimum of two standard cameras. Standard cameras in the market include; Nikon, Olympus, and Cannon. Nikon ranks high in the photography industry and is reputable for taking portrait photographs particularly, Nikon D7100.

You can get the higher version of Nikon to cover events, and the cost range of Nikon D610 is $1,900 while Nikon D7100 is about $1,250. Total = $3,150

IV. Cost of camera lenses

Naturally, cameras do not come with good quality camera lenses, so you must from the outset buy two different lenses for the two cameras. Since it has been suggested that you buy Nikon cameras, it is hereby recommended that you buy Nikon 35mm f/2.0 and Nikon 50mm f/1.8 for portrait cameras. The cost of Nikon 35mm f/2.0 is about $400 while the cost of Nikon 50mm f/1.8 is $350. Total =$750

V. Cost of computer systems and accessories

There is a need to acquire a durable computer system, and most systems are including Dell. The price of different brands varies, and a budget of $1,200 is not on the high side. There is also the need for a Photoshop program to be used in treating pictures. The price of $120 can be allocated for it while back-up hard drive of about $90 is just ideal. The total cost of computer systems and hard drive = $1,410.

VI. Website cost

In a photography business, a website is of necessity since your business is promoted and attract custom from a website and other social media platforms. The website is where potential customers/visitors go to assess your fitness for the job including looking at the photographs displayed on your site. Building an online presence is very important for any individual with the desire and goal to establish a successful photography business. In the light of this, a budget of $680 is just ideal including the annual hosting of your domain name of $80. Total = $680

VII. Other expenditures

You must begin to make provisions for launching your new photography business including promoting it until the initial acceptance is gained. To this end, there is the need to budget for business cards, flyers and advertisement placement in the electronic, print and online media. The budget for this depends on how big you plan the promotion blitz. Depending on the potential business in the target market, you may be budgeting $450 for promotion. Total = $450

Summary of the initial budget to launch your photography business:

1)   Business registration and insurance cover = $680

2)   Cost of a studio and renting facility =$2,150

3)   Cost of two standard cameras =$3,150

4)   Cost of camera lenses = $750

5)   Cost of computer systems and accessories = $1,410

6)   Cost of website =$680

Other expenditures =$450

However, the cost arrived at is estimated and doesn't represent the actual cost to be incurred if you decide to go into photography business today or next year. It is recognized that inflation cost, the business environment changes and the US State for your operation may determine the exact cost for your business. So, if you decide to go into the business, it is recommended that you carry out further market research including window shopping, to determine in more concrete terms the amount for your budget.

CHAPTER FIVE

First Steps into Photography

Now we have come this far, and I will introduce you to the actual business of photography. To go into the business, make sure you have undergone a period of training in a well-equipped studio and master the art very well before venturing into the business. If you want your photography business to be successful, make a profit and grow over time, do follow the following steps:

1. Name your photography business

The name given to your photography business may be your personal names such as Edward Christie Photography or something more unique that do not contain your personal name. You might want to find out whether the name chosen is available or has been taken. If this is settled, let us move to the next stage.

2. Create a logo for your photography business

Your logo design should capture the business you are in. Your logo should reflect the name of your photography business; the choice of a good logo should not pose a problem. A logo may consist of artistic designs, letters or just an admirable picture. It could be simple as anything, but make sure it showcases your uniqueness. If your focus is on events photography, your logo can be colorful that appeal to families.

3. Place of work for your photography business

The nature of your photography business determines your domicile for your business. If you are shooting events, i.e., focusing on outdoor and wedding shoots, working from home is an ideal place to work, but if you are going to set up a studio, definitely, you need to lease an apartment, paying rent and utilities.

4. Shareholders of the photography business.

If your photography business is solely owned, then decision making is relatively going to be simple. But if you are going to have other stakeholders such as investors and non-executive directors, or even staff members that are going to work with you, you will need to fashion out each person's role in the photography business. Naturally, legal contracts will have to be drawn, defining each person role in the business.

5. Choose your Niche

Which area of photography business you want to specialize, that depends largely on your training, skills, and equipment. It is advisable to focus on the area you are familiar and gradually diversify when your business begins to expand and make a profit.

6. How much to charge your clients for your services

First things first, find out the competitors' rates and take a cue from them. Don't forget that the rate you charge can vary with your skill and experience in the business. Focus on what your competitors charge and take an average of it.

7. Install an accounting software

Choose an application package that will enable you to track your income and expenses as well as compute your tax returns.

8. Brand and market your service products

Your service products must have a brand name for identification and to differentiate them from competitors service products. The manner of your dressing, the service quality as well as your final product, should reflect your brand. Here I refer to:

1) Your business cards

2) Your letterhead

3) Your slogan

To reach your target audience, your marketing promotion should be a mixture of:

1) Networking – reach other people from whom you know

2) Word of mouth marketing – via satisfied clients.

3)   Targeted social media – paid and unpaid

Now that you have completed the planning stage, it is time to go into the photography business proper. This entails the following procedure.

1. Register your photography business

You must follow the due process to get your photography business ready for operation.

2. Open a business bank account

This will enable you to keep track of your photography business finances.

3. Create your business social pages/platforms

1)   Create your Facebook business page, with the company profile picture in place to enable prospective clients to see who the photography business owner is.

2)   Create your company's other social media handle such as Instagram, Pinterest, and Twitter.

4. Start a blog on photography

If you want your business noticed by prospective clients, you must start a photography blog where you upload your photographs with text-tags. You don't need to write much since picture speaks better. But make sure you use the right keyword combination so people will find you when they search you using various search engines.

5. Create your booking checklist

This ensures that your client's business with you can be traced and ensures consistent delivery of quality images, hard copies and soft copies.

6. Create information sheets for your photo shoots options

These information sheets will cover various shoot options, frequently asked questions (FAQ) such as outfit guidelines, best moments to do certain shots as well as what to bring along for the shoots.

7. Display your business with all important information

Make sure your address and contact information is conspicuously displayed on both website and your blog to enable people who love your work to communicate with you, and thus create more opportunities and exposure.

8. Have a referral reward system

This is a strategy to increase your sales at the start-up year, and if it is economically viable, the strategy has the potential for growing your business in the year of launch.

9. Be professional in your photography business

Treat every client with the curtsey it deserves. You can communicate in semi-formal, thereby avoid the use of chatting language you see on SMS or WhatsApp.

CHAPTER SIX

How To Expand Your Business

How to expand:

1. **Be an entrepreneur:**

   The photographer should exhibit some level of professionalism if he is to deliver value to customers at all times. He/she must possess the qualities below: -

   - Timekeeping - Deliver work on schedule and keep an appointment
   - Personal appearance - mode of dressing, dress to attract custom as well as being noticed.
   - Human relations -- Get along with your customers.
   - Enthusiasm - Have an interest in your business and be a master of it all.
   - Co-operation - with members of your staff.
   - Receptiveness - to new ideas and photography techniques.

2. **Have an annual business plan**

Articulate what you are going to do in the next six months to one year and make sure you follow it to the letter. Incorporate in the plan the areas of the business you want to see expanded, such as opening a new branch office, employing one or two assistants, launching into a new niche or new market. The business plan will guide you on what to do and when to do it.

3. Have an attractive website

Your website is like shop front where you display samples of the work and background information of your business, so get your website's color and layout to be simple and elegant, to wow consumers and to make them come back.

4. Be involved in social media marketing

If you are going to promote your photography business, social media is the best and cheapest place to go because it is possible to display your brands on the social media as well as display the social media icons on your website. You can also join social media groups and promote your brands on those platforms. Apart from posting your brands of work, it is also possible that you engage a professional graphic designer to create attractive media content for your photography business.

5. Expand your network of different groups

These groups include customers, business associates and other people engaged in the business of photography. They may offer genuine assistance in the way of expert advice, referrals and much more. It is also possible to expand your network by being part of photography networking, attending seminars organized by photography group and other events involving photo shoots. Photography events like exhibitions are another area you can explore, either you organize it on your own or attend the one organized by the network you belong to. Be sure you add the attendees to your network

6. Promote your photography business consistently – ways to do it:

Create value for your potential customers

You can do this by leveraging on content marketing, i.e., creating a piece of material or content that may be in the form of video or blog post that answers someone's question or solve a problem that is frequently asked.

Do a collaboration shot

You can do this by creating new connections, share and tag each other so that audience of those you have the connection with maybe your audience and theirs your audience.

- Link up with a charity organization

You can team up with a charity to get noticed. Find out about the charity around your community that you can team up with to get your photography business. The important thing here is that you can snap good photographs of the charity free of charge and your business can be noticed. Don't forget that your photograph on this charity will be seen on the charity's website, so also you can share the photograph on your blog.

CHAPTER SEVEN

How To Hire The Right Assistance

To engage the right assistance, there is a need for job description and job analysis. These are statements of facts describing the work to be performed, the responsibilities involved, the skills and training required, the conditions under which the job is to be done and the relationship with other jobs.

A job description would show the following

- Job summary – showing in a few paragraphs the major functions and tools used in performing the job of a photographer assistance

- Job content – lists the sequence of operations that constitute the job, i.e., leading to a perfect picture being obtained

- Statement showing the relation of a job to other closely associated jobs.

- Training required, working hours and peculiar conditions of employment

Personnel specification:

This refers to the personal characteristics required to do a job, e.g., photographer skill/experience and special aptitudes. Personnel specification would also show the following:

Sex, age and physical characteristics required, e.g., size, energy level, mental ability, and emotional maturity, cultural requirements, e.g. speech experience and skill needed.

Summary of Procedure for Recruitment and Selection of photographer assistance

I. A staff requisition form- This is required to be completed by the head of the department where the vacancy arises
II. An advertisement is placed.
III. Shortlist is drawn up, and an interview is arranged
IV. References – this can be taken up before the interviews and used to

determine the final selection at the interview.

V.   Interviews are conducted including tests for specific skill

VI.   Medical examinations are taken

VII.   Unsuccessful candidates have notified

VIII.   Successful candidates are informed and records updated.

However, before you can hire an assistant, you must find out whether you need one and cash is available to pay salaries at the end of the week/month. Perform a business vs. workspace analysis, and you will figure out the need for assistance.

- Do you wear out at the end of a normal day work?
- Do you complete tasks that need to be completed every day?
- Do you think your relationship with your family and friends are beginning to suffer?
- Are your other employees complaining that you are pushing

work that is not related to their engagements?

- Are you contemplating slowing down the growth of your business to keep yourself from being consumed by the work?

How to hire the right assistant for your photography business

- **Do proper job analysis and man profile before advertising the position**

When you post the position, make sure you know exactly what job the assistant will do when employed. Set the educational requirements and on the experience required. Are the duties fall into one or all these: taking inbound and outbound telephone calls, taking care of the business social media platforms, scheduling meetings for the CEO, arranging travel and accommodation and filing appropriate tax returns. Also, the length of training required before he/she will begin to be productive. If the assistant, however, is going to take up more complex jobs, then he/she may be entitled to a higher payment.

- **Don't limit the channels for seeking for the right candidate**

All possible channels must be explored. Speak to your photography association friends, social media groups, personal contact with people who know better. You will always be open where there is potential for recruiting assistants such as places where different people take photographs either for business or personal use.

- Don't be desperate or in a hurry to engage an assistant because if you are to employ the wrong person, it is likely you will rush to sack the So it will be a good idea to slow down in your effort to employ an assistant.
- Screen out candidates that do not fit into your company culture

The candidates may all be competing for the job, but if they do not fit into the company's culture, i.e., the way of doing business in your photography business, then they can't be engaged.

- **Screen them on how they take the initiative and their energy level**

If the assistant is going to hold brief for you when you are away, then he/she is to be well groomed for the job. This is where age and maturity are important. Here you must engage not only someone who is professionally qualified but someone who is also emotionally matured. Find out the greatest job the applicant has ever undertaken, from the responses; you will be in a position to fire further questions. You want someone that can replace you whenever you have to go out of town – you will have a chance to create time for other important things while they handle your business.

- **Use leading questions to expose any serious flaws they may have**

When you screen possible candidates for jobs, do not always look at their positive sides, also look at the other side because one major negative action, such as stealing, will ruin your photography business. Sometimes, it may not be stealing your equipment, but refusing to obey your instructions.

- **Make them partake in a practical project**

The areas they have the knowledge, conduct a sample test on each of the applicants, this will expose some of them to the areas they claim they have the knowledge, either their knowledge is limited, or they don't have it at all. Don't be in a hurry to take on an assistant; the time wasted at this stage is worth it. Otherwise, it will backfire.

- **Make sure you take what referees say seriously**

Referees can give you vital information on an applicant past work history or their characteristics, whatever, the information is important before you do the final selection. The report might be that the applicant doesn't take his job seriously, or that he doesn't take instructions, or that he submits reports late.

- **Allowed the applicant some time to ponder over the job offer**

You are engaging an assistant because you are taking too much work upon yourself and need to reduce the workload. The applicant may not like the job offer after all, but if you insist on him resuming work immediately, he might just work for a few days/weeks and throw in the towel.

- **The job applicant is now an employee**

The first thing you do on engaging as an assistant is to start training him/her on work standard of your photography business. Show him everything on a step-by-step basis and give him ample opportunity to learn by asking questions concerning his job.

- **Make your expectations known to the assistant**

You must communicate to the assistant in clear terms what your expectations are and watch over him to make him fall in line. If he doesn't, it is your duty to coach him/her to make sure the job is performed. If the assistant doesn't perform within a specified period, you may have committed a blunder to have deemed it fit to engage such an incompetent person.

- **Get regular feedback from your assistant**

It is absolutely necessary to ask for feedback whenever work is assigned to the assistant. The performance of the assistant job should be monitored until completion and assistance given to him where necessary.

CHAPTER EIGHT

Best Location for Your Photo Studios

It is vital that a photographer should have a photo studio to shoot portraits of customers, their friends, and family members. When choosing the perfect location for your photography business, there are important factors to be considered.

Understanding where, why, and what target customers consider before approaching a photo studio is the first step in finding a suitable place to site your studio. The photographer must understand the service output levels desired by the target customers, a convenience place for customers' waiting to be served, parking lots for customers, place that is safe for customers to come and go, and more importantly, the place that is suitable for the photographer to do his business and make profit. So, if many couples use a particular court for their wedding, use a possible location near the court; if there are fashion houses around a particular location or even a holiday resort, fix your studio close to the area since people in the area will have a great need for a photographer sometimes.

1. Know what you want for your photography business.

When you set up your studio business, talk to yourself to know the kind of studio that will suit you. Consider how big your photography business should be, the studio space required, a number of people to employ, types of equipment needed and whether there is the need for future expansion.

2. Photographer's convenience

It is absolutely important that the photographer should not have problems going into his studio at all times. The photographer should not locate his studio where it will take him hours to reach his studio because of traffic-related issues or locate his studio in an estate that has restrictions on the use of the facilities of the estate.

3. Human traffic

It is recommended that studios should be located where there is a high volume of traffic of people and a location that does business 24 hours, seven days a week. The simple reason that photographer customers can do business at any time and you will have no reason not to attend to them. Secondly, crowded areas are better; simply because even without heavy promotion to announce your presence, people will see you so far, your signboard is conspicuous enough.

4. Well-Known locations

No all locations are reputable, some locations are well known, and people do not have problems visiting such places.

5. Choose a location where you get natural light.

Every photographer has a lighting system, but the natural light will appear to be a better alternative. So, choose a location where there is a natural reflection of the natural light so that you use it during the day.

6. **Consider expanding your studio in the future.**

   Choose a location that allows leeway to expand in the future if your business grows in the future and you want to expand. Some locations are choked up already and no more room for expansion, the only alternative then is to relocate.

We have looked at locations to fix your photography studio, let us also look for a perfect outdoor place to shoot your photographs

1. Look for a location that has shelter nearby for the obvious reasons that the weather may suddenly change. If you choose an open place far from

shelter, and it happens to rain, there is much to lose than gain.

2. Choose a quiet location Places that is overcrowded like big cities, and public parks are not very suitable for taking outdoor photographs. You will keep on adjusting, waiting for people who move about to stop, which is impossible. However, choosing a busy location, there is the possibility of getting a few inquiries from passers-by.

- **Environmental impact on location decision.**

   Some shoots are better done in leafy green environments because of the freshness and wholesome looks it brings. Others would prefer sandy beaches, while others would prefer the golden hues of autumnal forests because it is really cozy for families.

1. **Different things in one place.**

   Some photographers don't it find funny moving around from one point to another while engaged in a long shooting exercise since it is likely to disrupt the free flow of the shoot and people having to move to another location. It is a lot of work on the part of the photographer since he has to arrange and convey his equipment to another location.

2. Private and public places

Some places are not open to the public and in some places that the public are permitted, shoots may not be allowed.

3. Peoples' safety

Wherever you choose for your outdoor photograph, your subjects' safety should be a major consideration. So, it means that you should find a location that will ensure that your subjects are safe when they are at the scene of the shoot.

By and large, we have looked at a location where you can site your studio as well as your outdoor location. The question is, how do you find your perfect location, both for studio and outdoor shoots.

1. Research the web

    Use Google map to browse the internet to locate places where you set up your studio or do an outdoor shooting.

2. Ask friends and associates, including social media groups, particularly those in photography business where you can find a suitable site

3. Look for unoccupied stores.

    Visit the vacant stores and figure out whether it will suit your photography business, and whether it will serve your purpose, contact the owner, if suitable.

4. Consult an Estate Agent

An estate expert will not only advise you on where to find suitable accommodation for your photography business but will also advise you one safety of the area, human traffic level and whether it is a good business area.

CHAPTER NINE

Pitfalls to Avoid in Photography Business

1. Not using the right kit to complement your expensive camera.

It happens to a lot of photographers who think what matters is the camera only. If you fail to support your camera with good lenses, you cannot get the best from your camera

2. Not paying attention to little things

Not have spare batteries in the hope that the battery in your camera can carry you through an event, only for the battery to discharge in the middle of the event. Or for you to run out of your storage space, or camera to develop an unforeseen fault. Always have double of all those things that can disappoint you without notice.

3. Not keeping your kits clean

For a camera to shoot and you get the best result, it must be professionally maintained. Though today's cameras have built-in sensor-cleaning mechanism, it is possible that this cannot remove the stubborn dirt. You can get the sensor cleaning kit do it yourself (DIY), or you can invest in getting a professional clean it every six months. Failure to take care of your camera this way, the image of your pictures will seriously be affected. Many camera dealers offer this cleaning service.

4. Failure to locate the venue of an even beforehand

It might sound simple, but you cannot quantify the loss to a photographer who arrives toward the closing ceremony of a wedding service, how the couple would be devastated especially if they could not find an alternative photographer.

5. The danger of copying another photographer's style

As a photographer, you must be identified with your unique style, your unique selling proposition; that style that makes you stand out from the crowd. It is advisable to have your style instead of copying someone else's. There is always something that makes you stand out. Focus on the unique part of your skill, and you will be inspired to create a greater piece.

6. Your camera is not handy

As a photographer, you must have your camera handy even if you don't plan to snap while on an outing, but who knows, an opportunity may arise for you to take photos of your subjects who happen to be at the right place at the right time. So have a camera handy as you go out even the pocket-sized one that can craft creative images, with even a low noise and shallow depth of field.

7. Relying heavily on the image-editing process

Photographers often make the mistake of not getting the exposure level right as the object is shot, but relies on getting it right when the processing takes place. The point is that the processing cannot help either.

8. Never give up in a hurry

Sometimes, it may look as if you have failed as a photographer because equipment does not function the way it should, the weather is not good enough to snapshots, the movement of people at a place you a taking photos, or it would appear you are not making headway in the business of photography. Don't quit, persevere, in the end, you will be a winner.

CHAPTER TEN

Conclusion

To go into photography business and succeed, you need to have the passion and perseverance and put in your best efforts. Those who thrive in this business is not by chance; you will be surprised when you hear their success stories and what makes them thick. No matter how proficient you are in the photography business, there are the downsides of the business.

1) Equipment breakdown – laptop malfunctioning or camera flash fails to work.

2) Mutual and common mistakes on taking instructions from the client

3) You can trip and slip on negotiating to take a shoot.

4) The quality of pictures may be short of client needs.

5) You may miss to deliver before the deadline or fail to keep an appointment.

Photography business, like any other business, requires passion and perseverance to succeed. You must love what you are doing, be determined to succeed, and put in your best; you will receive your reward. You must site your studio in a place right for your business, always try to grow your business by looking for new opportunities, employing and training your staff. However, some pitfalls are inevitable and even sometimes unavoidable, just work to the best of your ability, and you will have stories of success to tell.